DARING MISSIONS IN MATH

VENOM COLLECTORS

Kelli Hicks

Cherry Lake Press

Published in the United States of America by Cherry Lake Publishing Group

Ann Arbor, Michigan

www.cherrylakepublishing.com

Reading Adviser: Beth Walker Gambro, MS, Ed., Reading Consultant, Yorkville, IL

Photo Credits:
Cover © Lauren Suryanata/Shutterstock, (snake), © Ali _Cobanoglu/Shutterstock, (inset photo), © ranjith ravindran/Shutterstock, Folder graphic, (bottom right), Cover; © ranjith ravindran/Shutterstock, (Folder), © iSKYDANCER/Shutterstock, (spider), page 4; © sundatoon/Shutterstock, (cartoon snake), © sundatoon/Shutterstock, (cartoon snake), © IrinaK/Shutterstock (scorpion), © Travis Potter/Shutterstock, (frog), page 5; © GOLFX/Shutterstock, page 6; © DSlight_photography/Shutterstock, page 7; © Tyrone Winfield/Shutterstock (large photo), © skorovik/Shutterstock, page 8; © bullyzuar adam innocentia/ Shutterstock, © Far700/Shutterstock, (equipment bag), page 9; © Anatoliy Cherkas/Shutterstock, page 10; © Caftor/Shutterstock, page 11; Credit Alex Holt/NIST, snail lab photos, pages 12 and 13; © Aha-Soft/ Shutterstock, ribbon illustration, page 12 and throughout book; © Ali _Cobanoglu/Shutterstock, page 14; Quang Vinh Tran/Shutterstock, (cobra illustrations in chart), © Kurit afshen/Shutterstock, (green pit viper), © chemical industry /Shutterstock, (vial of venom), page 15; © cynoclub/Shutterstock, (glass terrarium), © cynoclub /Shutterstock, (scorpions), page 16; © PeopleImages/Shutterstock, (inset photo at top), © Innerchild Studio/Shutterstock, (illustration of coins), © 24Novembers/Shutterstock, (scorpion), © ShishkinStudio/Shutterstock, (scientist holding tweezers), page 17; © Erin Donalson/ Shutterstock, pages 18-19; © Ken Griffiths/Shutterstock, page 21.

Produced for Cherry Lake Publishing by bluedooreducation.com

Cherry Lake Press is an imprint of Cherry Lake Publishing.

Library of Congress Cataloging-in-Publication Data has been filed and is available at catalog.loc.gov.

Printed in the United States of America

ABOUT THE AUTHOR

Kelli Hicks is a teacher, mom, and sports enthusiast who lives in Tampa, Florida. She is fascinated by the amazing research to find cures and treatments for health conditions. She is thankful there are brave heroes willing to take risks to help the medical community.

TABLE OF CONTENTS

MISSION FILE

Our mission is to extract highly toxic **venom** from various animals for research needed to save lives.

Fifteen percent of the world's animals produce venom. Venom can kill, and it works fast. Researchers have discovered that venom can also be used to save lives.

Black widow spider bites have been known to kill people.

Animals use venom to protect themselves from predators or to paralyze their prey. Using venom can also help animals protect their homes. This makes it easier for them to survive in the wild.

Venomous animals, such as scorpions, inject **toxins** into their victims. Poisonous animals are different. They deliver toxins to their victims through contact.

Scorpions have a stinger at the end of their tail. They use it to inject venom.

Do not touch poison dart frogs. They produce a toxin that covers their skin.

Venom from different animals can be used to treat and cure a number of health problems. Our team has a dangerous job. We need to handle these dangerous animals and carefully **extract** the venom.

Only experts should handle venomous or poisonous animals. The experts know the best and safest ways to handle them.

Team members need to understand how to read the body language of the animals to prevent injuries. Looking for signs of aggression, changes in eyes or head shape, **posture**, or fast tongue movement will keep us safe.

Understanding a snake's body language helps the experts know when it is about to attack.

MISSION PLAN

Our mission is at the research center. We will need sets of protective equipment for each animal we will work with.

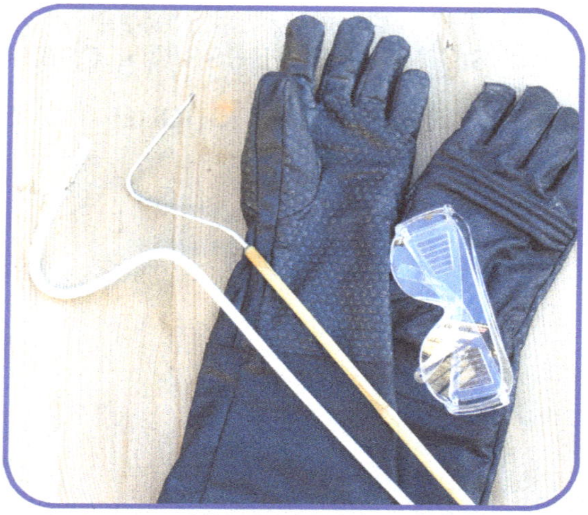

There are eight members in our team. Each team member needs six sets of equipment. There will be one for each animal we will work with and a spare set. How can we find out how many sets we will need?

Think About It!

To find out how many sets we need, we multiply the number of sets by the number of team members:

$$6 \times 8 = 48$$

Answer: We need 48 sets.

Challenge Yourself!

If we add 3 more sets to each pack, how many sets would we have all together?

KEEPING CALM

The research center has an apiary, a special place where bees are kept. Here, the researchers study how bee venom can be used for medical purposes. They believe the venom can be used to treat arthritis, but more research is needed.

This kind of venom collection needs special equipment. Researchers that work with the bees need a full bee suit, a veil to protect their faces, gloves, and a smoker.

The smoker releases a stream of smoke that actually calms the bees to prevent stings. Our team is delivering eight smokers to the research center. Each can burn for 5 hours. How many total hours of smoke can all eight smokers produce?

Think About It!

To find out how many total hours of smoke the smokers can produce, multiply the number of smokers times the number of hours each smoker will burn.

$$8 \times 5 = 40$$

Answer: The smokers can produce smoke for 40 hours.

Challenge Yourself!

If researchers burn 4 hours of smoke per day, how many days will the smokers last?

CAUTIOUS COLLECTIONS

At the research center, the first **lab** we enter has cone snails. The cone snail naturally lives in tropical waters. The cone snail is a deadly creature. It uses its **proboscis** to inject its stinging venom, which paralyzes its prey.

Cone snail venom research produced a medicine that can block pain in some patients.

Don't get too close! Using tongs, a researcher will grab the snails and add them to collecting trays. Each collecting tray can hold up to eight snails. Our team will prepare the trays. How many trays do we need to collect 24 snails?

Challenge Yourself!

How many trays do we need to collect 34 snails?

A team member holds a collection tube used to collect the deadly snail venom from its proboscis.

Our next job is at the research center's **serpentarium**. It has many different kinds of snakes. The research center needs to collect 600 milliliters (20 fluid ounces) of snake venom. It will be used to make **antivenom**. We need to figure out how long it will take to collect.

The research center collects 15 mL (0.5 fl oz) of venom per snake each month. If there are eight snakes, how much venom does the research center collect in 1 month? How many months will it take to collect 600 mL (20 fl oz)?

Researchers hold the snake by the neck and squeeze the venom into a container.

One Month

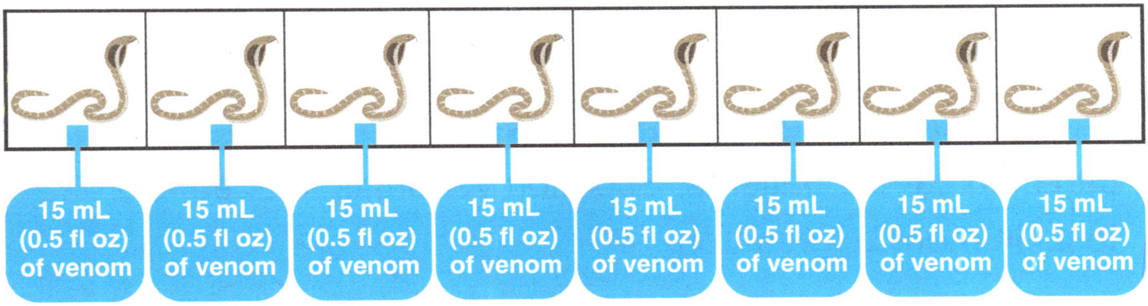

Challenge Yourself!

How much venom can be collected in one year?

Between 7,000 and 8,000 people in the U.S. are bitten by venomous snakes every year. Antivenom should be given as soon as possible. Most hospitals have antivenom for these emergencies.

green pit viper

We are called to another task. The lab reports that scorpion venom can help patients find relief from **inflammation**. There is also a possibility that the venom can help cancer patients. Scorpion venom is needed for tests in medical research.

Our team helps collect 200 mL (6.8 fl oz) of venom. If each medical test uses 5 mL (0.17 oz) of venom, how many tests can researchers now run?

Challenge Yourself!

How many mL (or fl oz) of venom will they need for 20 tests?

Some scorpion venoms contain a substance that can kill bacteria. This may lead to scientists making new antibiotics.

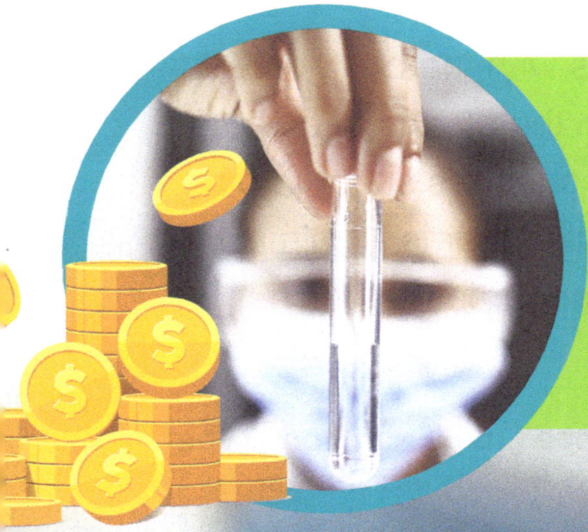

Scorpion venom may be the most expensive liquid in the world. It is extracted drop by drop. A quarter of a gallon (a liter) of scorpion venom is worth millions of dollars!

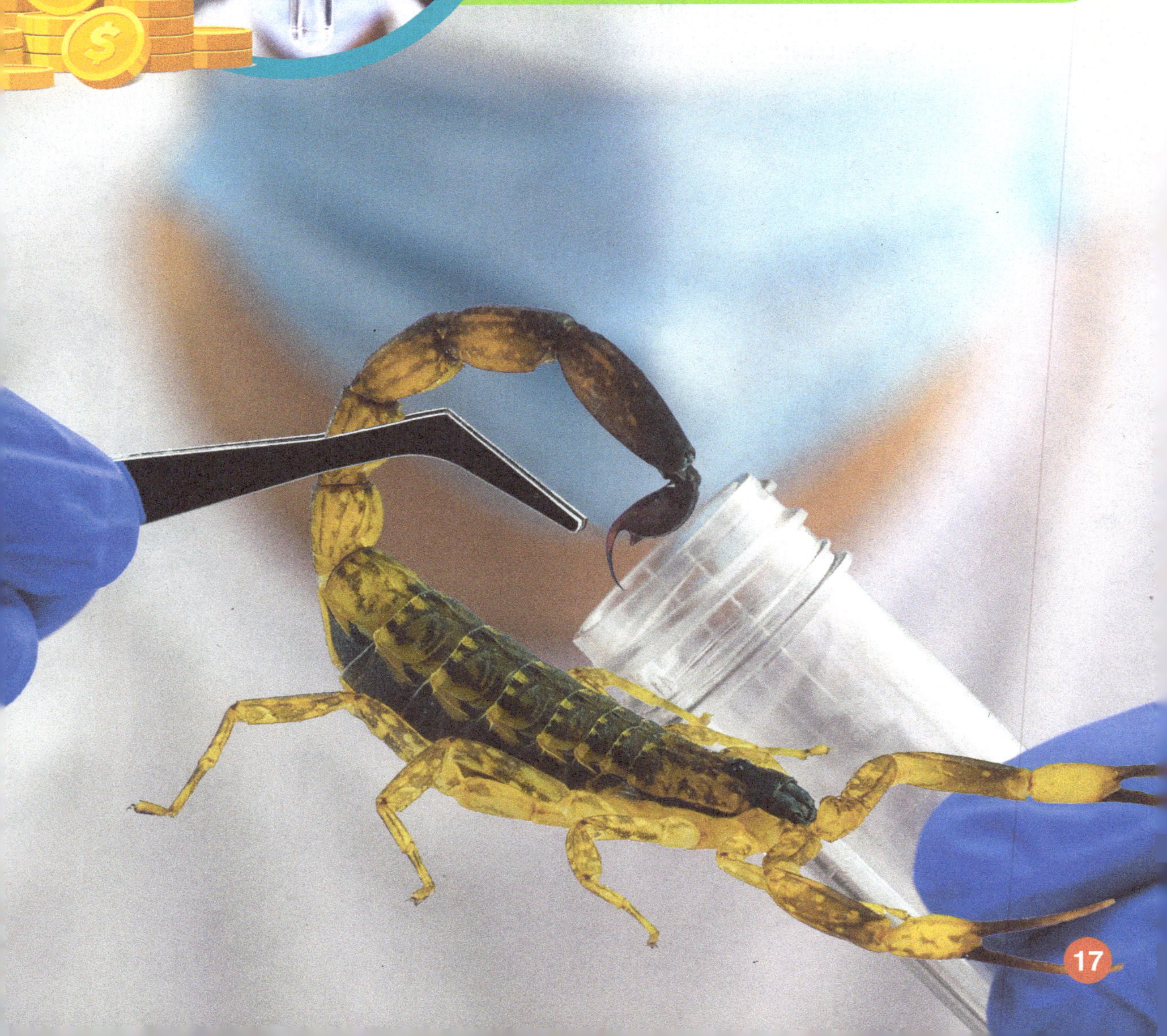

Our last venom collection stop is with the center's Gila monsters. Many people suffer from the effects of diabetes. This disease affects how the body changes sugar into energy. Venom from the Gila monster seems to mimic the way insulin works to help process sugar in the body.

Gila monsters are about 18 to 22 inches (46–56 cm) long. They are the only native venomous lizard in the United States.

The research center has 72 Gila monsters. A researcher assigns each team member the same number of Gila Monsters. How many Gila monsters will each team member work with? Remember, there are eight people on the team.

Challenge Yourself!

If each Gila monster can produce 20 mL (0.68 fl oz) of venom, how much venom can we help collect in total?

Research shows that a substance in Gila monster venom may help cure some brain diseases.

MISSION ACCOMPLISHED!

We collected enough venom for research without getting injured. The researchers can continue finding cures and treatments for many different illnesses.

The chart below shows how much venom one team member helped collect over 5 days. What is the total amount of venom one team member helped collect?

VENOM COLLECTIONS	
Type of Venom	Quantity
Bee	30 mL (1 fl oz)
Cone snail	30 mL (1 fl oz)
Gila monster	180 mL (6.09 fl oz)
Scorpion	25 mL (0.85)
Snake	30 mL (1 fl oz)

Challenge Yourself!

If each team member collected the same amount of venom for those 5 days, how much venom did the team collect?

Researchers continue to study venom from different animals. Their medical breakthroughs will provide new and **innovative** treatments for even more diseases.

The Australian funnel web spider is a deadly creature. Its venom can kill a human in as little as 15 minutes. However, researchers discovered a substance found in the venom can help to prevent brain damage caused by a stroke. What an amazing discovery!

Answers

Page 9: To find out how many sets we have if we add 3 to the pack, we first have to add the original number of sets with the additional sets: 6+3=9. Then, multiply the number of sets by the 8 team members. 9×8=72. **Answer:** There would be 72 sets total.

Page 11: To find out how many days the smokers can burn, we start with the number of hours of smoke we can make which is 40 hours. Then divide the number of hours by the number of hours researchers burn smoke per day. 40÷4=10. **Answer:** The smokers can burn for 10 days.

Page 13: To find out how many trays we need for 24 snails, we can divide. If each tray holds 8 snails, 24÷8=3. **Answer:** We need 3 trays.

To find out how many trays we need for 34 snails: 34÷8=4 with a remainder of 2 snails. **Answer:** We need 5 trays.

Page 14: To find out how how much venom we can collect in one month, we multiply the number of snakes by the amount of venom we can collect from each snake in one month: 8 snakes times 15 mL (0.5 fl oz) of venom. 8×15=120 mL (8×0.5 = 4.0 fl oz). **Answer:** 120 mL (4.0 fl oz).

To find out how long it will take to collect 600 mL, we divide 600 mL (20 fl oz) by 120 mL (4.0 fl oz). 600÷120=5 (20÷4.0=5). **Answer:** It will take 5 months to collect 600 mL (20 fl oz).

Page 15: Multiply the amount of venom collected in one month by 12: 120 mL (4.0 fl oz)×12=1,440 mL (48 fl oz). **Answer:** 1,440 mL (48 fl oz).

Page 16: To find out how many tests can be run, we need to divide the number of mL or fl oz by the number of tests. 200÷5=40 (6.8÷0.17=40). **Answer:** We can run 40 tests.

For the challenge, multiply the number of tests by how much venom is needed per test. 20 mL×5 mL=100 mL. (20 fl oz×0.17 fl oz=3.4 fl oz). **Answer:** We need 100 mL (3.4 fl oz) for 20 tests.

Page 19: To find out how many Gila monsters each person gets, divide the number of Gilas by the number of people. 72÷8=9. **Answer:** Each team member will get 9 Gila monsters.

For the challenge, multiply the number of Gilas by the amount of venom each can produce: 72 Gilas times 20 mL (0.68 fl oz) venom. 72×20=1,440 mL (72×0.68=48.96 fl oz). **Answer:** We can collect 1,440 mL (48.96 fl oz) of venom total.

Page 20: To find out how much venom one team member collected, add the amounts from each animal: 30+30+180+25+30=295 mL (1+1+6.09+0.85+1=9.94 fl oz). **Answer:** One team member collected 295 mL (9.94 fl oz).

For the challenge, multiply the amount of venom by the 8 team members. 295×8=2,360 mL (9.94×8=79.52 fl oz). **Answer:** The team collected 2,360 mL (79.52 fl oz) of venom in all.

Test Yourself

1. A group of researchers collect 650 mL (21.98 fl oz) of venom. If they collect 50 mL (1.69 fl oz) per day, how many days did they collect venom?
2. Researchers testing bee venom need 12 mL (0.4 fl oz) of venom for each experiment. If they have 132 mL (4.46 fl oz) of venom, how many experiments can they conduct?
3. A snake can produce 15 mL (0.5 fl oz) of venom per month. We collect the venom for 9 months. How much venom have we collected?
4. A tank can hold 6 scorpions. How many tanks will we need for an incoming collection of 87 scorpions?
5. The 20-inch (50.8 cm) bee smoker produces 10 hours of smoke before needing a recharge. If the team has 8 smokers, how many hours of smoke do they have?

Answers: 1. 13 2. 11 3. 135 mL (4.5 fl oz) 4. 15 5. 80

Find Out More

Books

Richards, Jon. *Calculations*, New York, NY: Enslow Publishing, 2026.

Singer, Marilyn. *Venom*, Mankato, MN: Lerner Publishing Group, 2020.

Websites

Search these online sources with an adult:

Division | IXL Learning

Venomous Animals | National Geographic Kids

Glossary

antivenom (an-tee-VEN-uhm) a special medicine used to fight the dangerous toxins from a bite or sting

extract (ek-STRAKT) to take or pull something out

inflammation (in-fluh-MAY-shuhn) redness, swelling, heat, and or pain usually caused by an injury or infection

innovative (in-uh-VAY-tiv) relating to a new idea or solution

lab (LAB) short for laboratory, a place used to conduct science experiments

paralyze (PAIR-uh-liez) to make something helpless or unable to move

posture (PAHS-chur) the position of the body

proboscis (pruh-BAH-sus) a long, tube-like mouth part

serpentarium (sur-puhnt-AIR-ee-uhm) a place where different types of snakes are kept

toxins (TAHKS-in) poisons

venom (VEN-uhm) a poison produced by some animals that is passed into victims through a bite or a sting

Index